Airs Above Ground

poems by

Jill Mceldowney

Finishing Line Press
Georgetown, Kentucky

Airs Above Ground

Copyright © 2018 by Jill Mceldowney
ISBN 978-1-63534-813-2 First Edition
All rights reserved under International and Pan-American Copyright Conventions.
No part of this book may be reproduced in any manner whatsoever without written permission from the publisher, except in the case of brief quotations embodied in critical articles and reviews.

ACKNOWLEDGMENTS

"Found" appeared in *Resevoir*
"Better Talk Now" appeared in *Oxidant Engine*
"Many Clouds" appeared in the *Nottingham Review*
"Terre à Terre" appeared in *Half Mystic*
"Mezzaire" appeared in *Half Mystic*
"Airs Above Ground" appeared in the *Sonora Review*
"Shared Belief" appeared in *Fugue*
"Paradise Woods" appeared in *Cosmanauts Avenue*
"Real Quiet" appeared in *Timber*
"Roses in May" appeared in *Harpoon Review*
"Hence" appeared in *Foothill Literary Journal*
"Blame" appeared in *Whiskey Island*
"Go For Wand" appeared in *Sidereal*

Publisher: Leah Maines
Editor: Christen Kincaid
Cover Art: *Love Each Other or Perish* by Alexandra Eldridge
Author Photo: Jensen Mceldowney
Cover Design: Leah Huete

Printed in the USA on acid-free paper.
Order online: www.finishinglinepress.com
also available on amazon.com

Author inquiries and mail orders:
Finishing Line Press
P. O. Box 1626
Georgetown, Kentucky 40324
U. S. A.

Table of Contents

Found 1

Better Talk Now 2

I Talk Matches in My Sleeplessness 3

Hence 4

Sunday Silence 5

Many Clouds 6

Airs Above Ground 7

Terre à Terre 8

Mezzaire 9

Shared Belief 10

Paradise Woods 11

Blame 12

Goodbye Halo 13

Different Winter 14

Real Quiet 16

Go for Wand 17

Genuine Risk 21

Roses in May 23

Found

I was a wall of teeth,

an intimacy only found when violence stops being
a game,
when I start asking for it.

Tie one end of a split extension cord to my tongue,
the other to that animal part of me,
that carrousel, that lights up to run

                      but always returns

to become a storm flag or the end of winter,
that month of ache,
that month of possible
to live
                                struck
                                like a pyre,

the almost no sound way my body makes a contest
out of impact:

                electroencephalogram,
                snow,
                jar of bees.

                Woman—

                I am better prepared for that surge of contact,
                of hand to body.

What I mean is
I thought I knew the silence
that goes on

                like a horse after the rider falls.

Better Talk Now

From the beginning, I tried to be nonviolent

> but this year's length is measured in trauma,
> the hound changed to wolf,

> to a scythe.

Speak
of the devil and he will shatter me at the good
car accident head trauma high.
The body acted upon is the body waiting to preform and

I take

> a fistful of your hair in that moth eaten hour against a chain link—

> *"Is this what a man does? Is this what a man does?"*

My giving—
> > exactly what I shouldn't
> > feels like

> *fuck it.*

There is still plenty of tonight, a part of me that deserves you,
that wants to

> hurt you like I want to hurt—

this into a love story.

I am just like the dog you have chained
to the front steps;

 this bitch bites, drags you in your sleep, sets you on fire.

I Talk Matches in My Sleeplessness

I think—
                fine.
                Alter me a little.

I could be animal natured, horse natured, you natured:

stranger,
come back stranger still.

Here, right here
in this house in the North—

       the most dangerous distraction is

a match,
an orchard,
the unsprung snare of my body.

Pardon my wild—
                my wild for you,
                my this for you,
                my very I for you.

Hence

—white horse went through the windshield of a car.
                              I thought it was a doe—

the *what* that lurched on fire
from the wreck. And what
must be said for the way that body fills with light as if to say: *follow*
    I think the path is this way—

Only a horse on fire understands
wanting something so badly and throwing your life away to get it.

Because who else would expect a woman
to fling herself into harm's way?
Who else?
What kind of animal lights her own hands on fire?

I am talking to myself
in the voice I would use to calm that burning horse: *"You're okay.
Quiet.*
        I will never leave you." Or I'm shouting *fire*—

I have been
changed.

In my blood shouting *blood*—

            are you calling to me white deer with no horns?

Must I die

to reach you—an ending that means
even if it only means
I have
        confused violence for passion—
        mistaken a horse for a deer?

Sunday Silence

It wasn't so much breaking a commandment—but you did break
my wrist in a Walmart parking lot.

I will put a romantic spin on this,
the bonechimes under my skin make a case for that
which I probably said:

"It's fine, I like your hair like that—be my executioner."

I was trying not to think of what my body might be doing,
The night split open—they call it shock.
They call it: *"What the fuck is happening to you?"*

—even Jesus was evasive during questioning.

The sparsity of the Gospels suggests He stayed silent
during the hours He hung there—that in the end even the Father
fled the scene of the crime, left the murder weapon,
the two by four used to break—

into a Honda Civic—
no car alarm—
the femurs of criminals.

All I know is what they give for pain:
a hacksaw, a lifetime of roadside graves,
bread & feathers &

"Thou shall not —"

I lied.
There was no trauma but this:

I fell from a horse,
broke
my fall with the heel of my palm—

What?

I said the bones broke themselves.

Many Clouds

keeping him a secret makes him inevitable and
you will do anything to avoid—

Ophelia forced
underwater in the neighbors' pond,
her cries of escape muffled by
her own hand over her mouth.

her doom,
you would avoid it
but the dead have you in their pocket.

before tonight,
you did not know that force provides such a force
that your head is vibrating with
someone laughing or coughing in

this land of ghosts and amulets where
the dead keep count.

you want to believe that the clock is meaningful,
that time's passing will bring you home—

but still, you have nothing to say to the night layered on night,
the blood spattered towel,
and where he rammed your head twice into the windshield of his car.

in that pitch—
wait forever

with your hands pressed to the side of your head.
all of your pain lives there,
takes you

by the hair. can you make sense
of what you know
was no mistake? never
speak, some things
are only true when they are spoken aloud.

Airs Above Ground

Teach me that old dance of the unexplained field,
that chest of alive where

a horse runs on alone.

I want to learn
or remember how

                                        to calmly go wild,
                                        to live

yellow eyed and perform

from shared memories of cavalry—
dressage,
that French for

                                        to suffer,

meaning
silence,

meaning shared window, shared kiss of blood.

Terre à Terre

I know the name of the first horse I own
is prophecy for the way I will die.

Are you that horse—
all the keys on a piano

                        played at once,

half child-half eaten

apple? Your teeth mark my future:

beaten water,
the rush imbedded swan,
radio waves—
rising, striking, rising,
struck

hive of
                    glass,

                  bees,

                  woman

face down in the water.

Now I feed you from my own palm,
a demonstration of faith.

Mezzaire

Slash the veil. Open
the sky so that I can go there.

Enough with

*can't follow horses
into the air*—we become

      like horses:

feel the earth by
the shape of the breath of it.

      Our horses become us:

hair, sweat, hard
lungfuls of air.

Shared Belief

If a horse kicks hard enough it can start a fire
and I have arrived at the dark part of my truth:
when arson looked profitable.

>We burned an entire stable to the ground.

I know, I know.
I've been cast as this victim, but—

Check the medicine cabinet.
It's called the compounds that make up narcotics shift over time,
>become something they're not—

>from the horses I learned this blunt force trauma.

You said burning to death feels like the flu
kicking you in the chest from the inside out.
Fire converts to fire
the thing it burns and
each day is a door I plunge out of
on fire—

>I want something I love to eat me alive.

I study myself in the mirror after I read my fortune in an apple—

>another nosebleed in my future,
>cardiac arrhythmia,
>accident,
>accident.

"Make it look like an accident—"

>like something
>an animal would do.

Paradise Woods

Say there is a ritual that will raise the dead.

I mean danger.
I mean divination—
that is what I am here for.

To begin
I need

                                      a volunteer,
                                      gunpowder, a rope,
                                      and only a mirror

can tell you what the dead are thinking.

I am a woman disguised as prey, cardinal, the bare of teeth. I am
the red fox,
tail set on fire
and turned loose
in the cherry orchard behind the house in the North.

                            Here, I once watched a fox and a horse,
                            both wounded during the hunt,
                            struggle toward dawn.
                            Their suffering was inevitable.

The horse stood trembling, had caught his leg in a toothed snare
intended for the fox,

and she limped on
three legs, smelling of gasoline, a book of matches
between her teeth.

Give
me the illusion of choice.
This is the fire I set myself
on fire—

Blame

This horse collides—another horse.
In the sky it is spontaneous combustion.
Here, it is called—
                     give your body to a ghost.

Power surge. Fade to—
                     if I blackout.

My blood has his voice.

He hands me a knife
no, needle—and
                     he hands me and he hands me—

put your hands on me.

Unlived, I should regret
                     calling this predestination or racehorse or it's not you it's—

'evidence of a struggle.'

But the best thing about Vicodin
is I can still feel its ghost in the clothes I wear.
Think acetylene torch. He and I—have you figured it out yet?
                     We are

                     playing horseshoes in our newly shaped bodies.
                     This looks so familiar.
                     This is the last time—

       "Let me fuck you while I pretend you are someone else."

Now laugh.
That's supposed to be funny.

Goodbye Halo

Saying no to something means saying—

yes,

I don't love you
here.
Here, I want to suffer

through a burning tire lot
to a river rising,
not river proper—
air and dream and turpentine.

You think I've been gone a short while.
I've been gone—
How long, Adonai? How long, Adonai?

I was sitting before a camera
I said like the Bible says:

"If you're watching this it means I'm already dead."

I wanted his hands
laying higher, higher,
too high—
not high enough.

I am that bitch
who climbed shamelessly from heaven,
the holy other. I wear a crown of gold barbed wire.

Say yes.

Say let's get good,
yes—in California,
both parties must sign off on the release.

Different Winter

We are never more intimate—
our body on body—we are
ice making ice,

our hipbones are scythes
our crude method of electrocution:
                      an extension cord split in half and

winter's long argument shoved up
against the refrigerator door.

        We will not exit this kitchen the same way we entered.

I have conquered my old need to flee. My body commits
to a different winter.

                      Do you really want to do this with me:

        a bell struck with open mouth desire
        is a simple aggravation,
                the ringing of your thoughts in your hands.

Your thoughts in your hands:

                Fight back. Fight back—

and I
use an old trick to train horses
that involves a bottle—

                              I break your jaw
with it. I mean
open wide open
across the kitchen floor.

Right there—
                    I love you so much I want to kill you.

I almost
don't stop—

Real Quiet

you would have his kind of magic:
horse tranquilizers cut with glass,
transubstantiation and—

"Is this your card?"

now disappear. the return is—
are you watching closely?

he will rough you up
will bake bread on the heat of your back.

you run your fingers down your own ribs.
think
greyhound.

it is love or it's—

he will put his hands on you to keep you.

you want a pillow to muffle your
want.

let's call a spade a

body that didn't ask for this
but is perfectly capable of rationalizing
that guilt is born out of necessity—
the night side of his teeth.

Go for Wand

We are the lovers who enter the woods.
Can we burn it down, I mean—

        burn it down?

I am dressed for immolation—

        the cycle of another desire, the glamour
of your name in my mouth.

Let me need to say it and still need you
to give me need.

Make me the darkest night of the year.

        Release me.

I know my way by touch.

Would you look only before you? Would you do this one thing for me?
Would you say the game that wants to be snared is the most difficult to
   capture?

I warned you
against forgetting
a lantern. Now—

        one of two things will happen: we will fall in love forever or

the answer is lonely
        even if a horse knows his own way home.

Pick a side,
time is not stopping.
The choice is making you
        and my shadow is fucking itself

between what I want and what I should
end against a wall
of North wind—awake—
where the vixen waits beneath a cherry tree,
to be hunted,
to be unmade—

her red,
her teeth—
              I hear the sound of your teeth against mine.

Don't talk to me about gentleness.
I never expected—
                      "*Possess me.*"

Yes,

I asked to be hunted and
oh yes, I am cunning. After all—I am here.
Love isn't all, isn't anything
           but impervious and lighting matches to swallow
           the flame, to control that which comes after;

the good business of my burning.

Let me get on with it.

Let me walk where all love ends,
in the garden where the devil grows her cherries.

                Love leads us

deep enough, tracks blood to the source, finds the devil at the treeline—

her kiss turns us animal.
Something with teeth

always lurks in a forest on fire
and no one wants to be
the one to put their hand into that predator's maw.

Suffering is inevitable.

I thought:

> *Holy.*

I thought:

> *So much blood—*

at the end

        of a love story,

the woods no longer a woods,
just heat and voices of the dead
almost deciphered—

        sound slows,
        accelerates,
        repeats.
        Images tick—

a horse jumps

        between flames and the heave of heat.

Once upon a—

            once

I imagined the future by feeling

my way through a house on fire,
like an animal sees at night.

Amazing I could be wrong
in any wrong when I call you to me,

to fire's deepest,

                        where the clock runs backwards.

Here, supposedly, is the truth it speaks:
                horse and arrow
                the fox is
                innocent enough,

all of this is love; this story of parted lovers everyone knows
the ending to

these bodies of flint.

Genuine Risk

If there is no beginning—
                                      okay then

                   no end.

Let me ascend.
Let me move again
                     as a wraith passing windows, all ways of

"*Yes—*"
I could yes

a new house, North, garden, orchard, from ash into being
right here
when the curtain rises, when what rises with it
waits for the hunter to forget—
                                      but don't

forget
my body dusted with the sex of fire,

so multiple and dazzled,
so—
                                        fuck
                                   palms against
the wall.

The nauseous shimmer of both
fox and horse on fire
rises to me.
Rise to me.

I know the story. I know fire

is probably ghosts
and ghosts always come back.

They say "No, this is a mistake—
get rid of it,

get rid of it all. Here,

let me help you."

Roses in May

he will stand over you with a pillow to hush you out.
he will tell you to sell your show horse,
because he knows what happened in the North—

and horses remind him of dead horses,

the head, the hooves, the silver stopwatch buried
and the body dragged to burn.

the cupboards empty.
the cupboards fill
a year of sleeplessness.

collapse to your knees. there are handsaws. there are shovels here.
meet him in the caves and he is red cut to collarbone.
still— he will kiss his way through moonless timber,
stride out into Kentucky.
there is a part of you looking straight at him
and the rest of you is trying to look away—

it is early May and someone is singing.

In addition to *Airs Above Ground* **Jill Mceldowney** is also the author of *Kisses Over Babylon* (dancing girl press). Her previously published work can be found in journals such *Vinyl, Fugue, Prairie Schooner, the Sonora Review, Half Mystic* and others. She is also a recent National Poetry Series Finalist. She currently resides in New Mexico where she works as an editor for Madhouse Press.

www.ingramcontent.com/pod-product-compliance
Lightning Source LLC
LaVergne TN
LVHW041521070426
835507LV00012B/1731